A SUCCESSFUL KINDLE PUBLISHING BLUEPRINT

LAUNCH AND PUBLISH YOUR FIRST BOOK, EARN PASSIVE INCOME AND CHANGE YOUR LIFE

By

CRAIG LEBOWSKI

Copyright © 2016

Table of Contents

Legal Notes

Read This First

Introduction

Chapter 1

Chapter 2

Chapter 3

Chapter 4

Chapter 5

Chapter 6

Chapter 7

Chapter 8

Chapter 9

Chapter 10

Bonus #1

Bonus #2

About The Author

LEGAL NOTES

Copyright 2016 – All Rights Reserved – Craig Lebowski

ALL RIGHTS RESERVED. No part of this publication may be reproduced or transmitted in any form whatsoever, electronic, or mechanical, including photocopying, recording, or by any informational storage or retrieval system without express written, dated, and signed permission from the author.

DISCLAIMER: The information contained in this book, and its complementary bonuses, are meant to serve as a comprehensive collection of time-tested and proven strategies that the author of this book has applied to earn extra income. Summaries, strategies, tips and tricks are only recommendations by the author, and reading this book does not guarantee that one's results will exactly mirror the author's own results. The author of this book has made all reasonable efforts to provide current and accurate information for the readers of this book. The author will not be held liable for any unintentional errors or omissions that may be found.

The material in this book may include information, products, or services by third parties. Third Party materials comprise of the products and opinions expressed by their owners. As such, the author of this book does not assume responsibility or liability for any Third Party Material or opinions.

The publication of such Third Party materials does not constitute the author's guarantee of any information, instruction, opinion, products or services contained within the Third Party Material. Use of recommended Third Party Material does not guarantee that your results will mirror those of the author. Publication of such Third Party Material is simply a recommendation and expression of the author's own opinion of that material.

Great effort has been exerted to safeguard the accuracy of this writing. Opinions expressed in this book have been formulated as a result of both personal experience, as well as the experiences of others.

INTRODUCTION

Hello there. It's safe to assume that by picking up this small guide you're interested in a career that involves writing in some form, or at least learn to make some money on the side in some way, and want to be successful, correct?

If the answer is yes, then perfect. This entire guide will help you with that and at least give you a basic understanding of what it takes to be successful in that regard. Not to mention how it can also help you go from making exactly $0 with your writing to at least something a little bit better for your bank account.

Now writing on an online medium is actually a wonderful and fully viable career that is available to practically anyone as long as you have an internet connection. After all, almost all communication is done through the medium of text. E-mails, instant messages, blog commentary, and even most social media are all done via text. Reading is one of the biggest staples of human communication and it's only increased exponentially thanks to the advent of the internet.

However, the problem is not everyone can write well. Writing is a skill like anything else in life that takes time to master and calls for a certain level of dedication to improve on. While literacy rates in the United States and other Westernized, Industrial are at an all-time high and illiteracy is a trait that's uncommon, even in developing nations, understanding is not the same as being good at it. Anyone can read and comprehend the words that they see after all, but some people aren't able to formulate them into a coherent sentence and tend to forget the fundamental rules of grammar.

Not only that but people, even in this new digital age, love to read books. While there's a lot of jobs out there that require writing in another capacity, a large number of people still purchase books on a daily basis.

So you don't need a fancy degree, you don't need any specialized training, and you certainly don't need to study and earn a certificate to be an excellent writer. All you need to be successful is a basic understanding of good grammar, how to plot and outline a composition, and internet access. The internet access is one of the most important bits for working on the internet after all.

With that said though there's a little bit more that goes into the making of a successful writer who publishes via the internet. I know that previously just a second ago I said all you need is good grammar and the internet, but that's just the requirements. To truly be success you have to have a certain level of dedication as well to the craft, and you have to understand the reality of being an Internet Writer as well.

The reality of it is simply this: For the most part you won't be making a lot of money at this. Not enough to be considered "rich"

For a hobbyist who simply wants to work on the internet part time to bring some extra income, this might not be a bad idea. What's an extra $100 to $200 a month to someone who works full time and only writes on the side as a hobby for fun?

For someone who's looking to make a career out of writing though it's going to be much harder. While it's true there are some writers out there who have struck it rich and made a lot of money off of their writing, those are only isolated incidents of success. For every one writer who made over $1 million, there are roughly 5,000 other writers who make enough to survive and put some away for retirement.

That's not to say that you'll continually be starving and broke. Like with any other profession in life you'll have you have to live within your means. This is more or less a warning to scare off the people who think that this will be easy and that they'll be writing scripts in Hollywood and living in mansions.

If you're still with me on this, perfect. Then the rest of this guide will surely help you out.

All of the information in here was designed to help you, the reader, out. And if you're still here with me after the first chapter, we'll be discussing how to get started. What this book will cover though is one of the most proven, and best, methods for internet writers who wish to produce works that will make some decent money. However, it's a lot more than just going in, putting an internet file out there and hoping for the best and that money will start flowing in from people who are just buying whatever you make. It takes a lot of time, dedication, and effort to start seeing true success, as has been mentioned before.

So, let's get started, and let's start learning about Kindle Publishing, as learning it straight off the bat is a good starting point.

For any other source of writing income, please look into my other e-books and guides.

Say Bye-Bye To Your day Job In 30 Days:

How I Make $5000 Or More Per Month In Passive Income Working From Home

Amazon FBA Blueprint:

How To Launch A Private Label Empire, Build A Six-Figure Passive Income And Achieve Financial Freedom

CHAPTER 1

WHAT IS KINDLE PUBLISHING EXACTLY?

Kindle Publishing, Also known as "Kindle Direct Publishing" is a part of the Amazon.com's business empire and is the e-book publishing part of the company that was released back in 2007 as a way to meet the demand of the growing electronic book market that was emerging with the Kindle, iPhones, and other growing tablets or specialized readers.

Essentially, what it is exactly is a format that allows publishers to bypass traditional publishing routes to publishing their books their way without the hassle of having to find a publisher and go through them. With Kindle Direct Publishing, you make sure your files are in the proper formats, have a decent cover to them as well as basic copyright information tagged in, and Amazon practically does the rest for you as they market it on their website to new readers who might be interested in your book. It's all pretty painless when you really consider it.

Of course, you might be asking yourself: What does Amazon get out of it if they're doing a bit of the work marketing it? The answer to that is that Amazon takes a part of the royalties from the sales of the e-books that are published and sold, which can be often as high as 65% depending on your options.

Though that's the great thing, and the worst thing, about Publishing on the Amazon Kindle format. When it comes to the options there are a lot of different ways that you can earn money with them dependent on your writing. Let's say you sit down, and decide that you want to make a series of Young Adult Novels, and publish them through various different methods, not just Amazon Kindle Direct. So you write it out, put it in a proper format, create an excellent cover, and market it (All topics to be discussed later), and you start getting revenue and attention. Under the Kindle Publishing options at its base, you can sell it through Amazon, as well as different publishers if you choose. However with Amazon Direct though if you go that route Amazon takes 65% of the sales, and the rest is split between you as the author, and any other publisher involved in the writing.

Now that seems like a lot, and there are other options to lower that in your favor. There's an exclusivity option where you can choose as the Author to give exclusive rights to Amazon for a short period. This means that whatever you write and publish on their format has to remain within their rights for a set period. You earn more on your sale this way, but you cannot legally sell it anywhere else. Of course, it's not permanent, and after the set amount of time for the exclusivity option to pass you can choose to extend it or not with Amazon. There are even options that you can choose to either make the book free for a certain number of days or join in on one of their many exclusive deals that bundle your e-book in packages to other buyers, where you earn a percentage of the profits.

And some of the best parts of publishing through the Kindle Format are that you can even set your own price from as low as $0.99 to as high as $200 if you feel your work deserves that much. While there are averages depending on the genre you're publishing, they're not fully set in stone and it isn't unheard of for some Authors to set their prices to match more traditional, physical copies of their book.

However, while this guide will continue to teach you as a new author the ins and out of marketing, developing, and creating your eBook, a few words of warning must be said. Legally, Amazon's contracts that you sign when you publish with them state that any sales that are conducted are as a licensing fee, and not a purchasing fee. This technically won't hurt you as an author as whoever purchases your books is allowed to read them, but for the customer that purchase from you, this means that they technically do not own your eBook, but are licensing it out. This means that anything you write technically belongs to you first, Amazon second, but have been known to also publish Authors who publish through multiple different formats.

However, if none of that bothers you and you simply want to just get started on writing books, and earning a decent income while you start your writing career then we can continue on. Because despite all of the faults of the Kindle Publishing format, it's still one of the best, and most solid ways for Authors to produce works and publish them while making money at it.

Chapter 2

Market Research

By continuing to read this guide, we're going to assume that you're still interested in wanting to publish through the Amazon Kindle Publishing format (hereafter called KDP Format), and that's a good thing.

So starting out, let's also assume that you have a few ideas on what you want to write. But where do you go from here? After all, it's not as easy as just putting words to a word document and then just publishing and letting the money roll in. You could technically do that, but you won't earn much income or recognition just doing that.

That's where Marketing Research comes in. What is Marketing Research exactly?

It's where you research the market.

However, it's not really just that easy. In a nutshell, it's a lot more than just typing into Google "What books make a lot of money" because you're going to get wildly different answers from many different authors. Plus you can't simply just mimic another author's path to success and hope for the best. Not only would you then be competition, but you'd also not get far as each different Authors path to success is different and dependent entirely on different circumstances.

Instead, this is where a little bit work comes into play. You could simply write about things that you like and subjects that you want to touch on, or write your fantasy epic right off the bat and publish that, though. In a lot of cases, especially starting out, that's actually recommended for new Authors as it gets them use to the KDP format, but for those authors who want to establish themselves as authorities over a given genre, marketing research allows them to find out what sections of different genres are both profitable, and in need of attention. This will allow you as an author to know what niche you can fill.

What is a niche you ask? In writing terms, a niche is a subset of a subset. A niche is more specialized than a genre in that it's almost a specific portion of that genre. Let's look at an example:

Let's say you're an author who enjoys fishing. Fishing is a very interesting topic to write about, as there are a lot of different people out there who enjoy fishing as a hobby. However just writing a book about "fishing" won't get you a whole lot of attention or sales. Upon further research, you find out there's a lot of e-book guides that tell you about fishing, but not enough about specific parts of fishing that people enjoy. So you decide that there aren't enough guides written on how to debone fish. There are plenty on how to catch fish, but nothing that talks about what to do after they have the fish or at least none that goes into detail.

So you've found a niche and decided to write several guides on how to properly store, debone, and preserve fish. Upon further specializing you decide that you want to write several different guides on how to do all of that with different types of fish, because not all of them take the same sort of skill to properly and safely debone, so you write guides on how to debone and store catfish, on how to debone and store pike, walleye, or even the differences between freshwater and seawater fish.

That's what Marketing Research does. It finds a hole in the publishing world that doesn't have enough attention to it and shows you where you can fill it up with your expertise.

But now, it is more than just knowing what niche you can easily fill, you have to know what words you can use to properly get noticed, which is discussed in the next chapter.

CHAPTER 3

KEYWORDS, KEYWORDS AND MORE KEYWORDS!

So you've gotten your niche that you're writing in, and you know what subject you want to start specializing in right off the bat. That's good, and the end of it, all right?

Yes and no.

Yes in that it's possible that you can just end your research there and write what you want and start to get noticed, but no in the fact that you need to know what sort of keywords to use to even get noticed.

Let me explain.

Keywords are words that are used to essentially be snagged out of a search engine that is tied to your book. We're not talking about words that are used all the time like "the" and "and" or any other broad termed words. This is all a part of what SEO (Search Engine Optimization) marketing is about, and while you don't need to be an SEO expert to know what needs to be written to catch attention, at least having a basic understanding of what SEO and keywords do can greatly impact attention to your books. Well-chosen keywords are often the difference between getting a sale and being noticed, and being obscure and not being noticed at all.

"So what?" you might be saying right now. "Couldn't I just use every available keyword to maximize exposure?" Theoretically, you could just use all kinds of keywords to tag yourself in search engines. That's certainly what a lot of people do when they start out, and it's easy enough to make that mistake. The more keywords you have, the more attention should be given to you when someone types up what they're looking for in the search engine. However, that's not really the case, as oversaturation of keywords can actually have detrimental effects on your placement in a search engine. Not only are you competing against other people, who do the same thing with their writing, but you also have to compete with a lot of other various different guides and eBooks and stories and whatnot that are competing with you that might not even be in the same category as you. You could have keywords that you use about your fishing guide that overlap with hunting, or stories about fishing, or scientific guides about fish, or even other wildly different topics that differ from what you're writing about.

Instead, it's suggested that a few select keywords should be used. Usually, the number is between 3-6 different keywords even though you can go up to seven, but it's often recommended that 4 keywords per 5,000 words is often the best unless you're writing fiction. For nonfiction writing, 4 keywords is often the best as it's nice and concise, and anyone who goes to look for your subject usually tries to keep their keyword count low anyways to be as specific as possible.

So, continuing with our fishing as an example, if you were to write a deboning guide, some possible keywords you'd use for your book would be: Deboning, Fish, Storage, Safety,

And that's really all you would need to be placed in the search engine on Amazon's KDP portion. While you could have other keywords and tags in your writing, it's still advised to keep them smaller and consistent with the subject matter. Not only will that help you become more specialized in your niche, but will also rank you higher in the search engine the more sales you have, and how much of an impression you make on potential buyers.

Though, that does lead into the next chapter to discuss how to also catch the eye of potential buyers as well.

CHAPTER 4

CRITERIA FOR A SUCCESSFUL BOOK COVER

So far you've been doing really well, and you have an idea of what you want to write about. You've chosen your topic, you've chosen your niche, and you've even got a set of keywords in place that you're sure will get you noticed when people go looking for your specific topic. You should be done, right? That should be plenty?

Not quite.

Research shows that with a lot of customers, they spend about between 3 to 4 seconds looking a listed book in the KPD page before moving on. That's really not a whole lot of time, especially if you've written up a nice description of the book itself to draw the customers in more. One of the few reasons that they'd even stick around further to read up on your product before making a purchase is either through positive reviews (which will be in a separate chapter later on), or because of the cover of your book.

It's true. A cover for your book is vastly important to your sales as any other aspect of the book itself. A well-made, appealing cover to your book not only draws in the eyes of your viewer and forces them to stop and extend the time they visit your page, it also "sells" your book in a visual way that written words cannot. No matter how well written your book is, and no matter how many pages of samples you've given, most people do not have the time to stop and read samples of your work before making a purchase, however people are highly visual and respond to visual stimuli, so if they see a well-done cover, it more often than not garners some forms of interest as being a visual stimuli.

So what's the difference between a successful cover and a non-successful cover?

Non-successful covers are covers that work against you. Often they use clashing fonts, clashing colors, are visually uninteresting or unappealing (maybe even revolting) and also appear lazy and unfinished. Essentially a non-successful cover is just something that is hard to look at and doesn't go with what you're trying to portray.

Successful covers by comparison though are more than just being the opposite of their unsuccessful counterparts. While to at least gain some interest you do need to have an appealing cover that looks nice, is visually interesting, doesn't clash, and is in tune with your subject matter, it takes a lot more than just being overall decent looking. To truly be successful, it's often advised that you have a cover that's not only unique in its design, but also thematic.

What's meant by thematic is that it depends on the type of book you're writing. If you're writing something that's nonfiction, a good, successful cover is something that's simple that includes iconography of what you're writing about. So your fishing guide should include images of fish, on the cover, use fonts and lettering that draws your attention to the images themselves and be clear, concise, and uncluttered. This conveys exactly what the subject matter is.

Likewise, if you're writing fictional works of arts, such as stories, poetry, or the like, you want to use imagery that evokes the imagination of your readers. Fiction writing is designed around using the reader's imagination, so images that are somewhat of a mystery, but thematically tied into your writing generally are what draws in attention. After all, everyone who wants a good story likes a good mystery, and if your cover can somehow convey what your story is about, without giving any part of the story away, it'll make them want to pick it up and see what your story is about.

So now you've got everything you need on hand. You've got your subject matter, your niche, your keywords, and now you're getting ready to create a cover that conveys what your book is about. It's time now to put all of that together, and actually, create your book.

CHAPTER 5

CREATING YOUR BOOK

This chapter assumes that you've not written your book just yet, and had been focused on not only researching the market you want to write in, but also researching what niche to write in, what keywords to use for your subject matter, and creating a cover to place as an image for your book as well.

Well, right now comes the meat of the work when it comes to publishing, and the most important step: Writing it out.

Luckily for you, there is a myriad of different tools for writing at your disposal. In all honesty, it's often said among people that have been working the KDP platform for a while that all you really need to get started is a good understanding of the native language you're writing in and internet access. Of course, we need a little bit more than that. If you have a computer, chances are it has some sort of text editing software already installed on it. For the Windows OS that includes at its base Wordpad and Notepad.

On their own Notepad and WordPad are pretty good for what they do. Notepad is the least resource intensive of the two programs and is perhaps the easiest one to work with. All you do is load it up, and type, and when you're done, save it. However, the problem with that is that Notepad only saves in .txt format, and does not allow for any formatting of the words. This means no bullet points, no underlining, intending, or anything else.

As a contrast, WordPad does allow for font formatting. it allows you bold words, italicized them, underline, strike through, and even allows you to change the font of what you're writing into any number of fonts already defaulted on the computer itself. It's a great starting point for any writer, and it does allow you to save files in .rft, .html, and even other forms of extensions saved on your computer.

However, there are more tools that you can utilize that will help. A lot more! They include different text editing software, proofreaders, grammar checkers, plagiarism detection software, and even word spinners. Let's break them down into different categories to discuss them.

Text Editing Software

For the most part, WordPad and Notepad are all most writers ever really need. Text files are easy to open through almost every computer operating system out there, and if you don't need formatting done the files are generally pretty small and never get too big. Likewise, Rich Text Format (.rtf) files allow for formatting and are also easily opened on almost all kinds of different computer systems.

But sometimes you need Text Editing Software that does more than just format words. Sometimes, especially in regards to writing, that's not creative, you need to easily be able to manipulate your manuscript a little bit better with tools that allow you to do that.

Such manipulations of the manuscript can be headers and footnotes, allow for different information columns to be created, or to create a table that separates information into something pleasing for the reader.

Not only that, but different text editors do different things as well.

One of the most popular and free Text Editing Software available right now is the open source project "Apache Openoffice". What it offers, besides its price, is a community that's driven to develop plugins that alter how the base program works. At its core, it works much the same as WordPad, but with several differences. One of the biggest differences being that it allows for the creation of headers, and endnotes that can either have different information on each page, or be used to create titles at the top, and page numbers at the bottom. Not only that but with a multitude of different plugins that are created by the community you can customize your Open Office program to do almost anything you want it to do.

By contrast, though one of the most widely used Text Editing Software is still Microsoft Word from the "Microsoft Office" series. Not only does it generally come bundled as a package when you buy a prebuilt computer from most shops, but it can handle and read a wide variety of different text formats that include traditional text, rich text files, and even open source formats that are supported by Open Office. The downside is that it's generally a major purchase and comes bundled with a lot of other programs with it, but additional tools never hurt to have around, and learning their use can even add to your skillset. After all, being a good writer and a successful writer requires more than just being able to type coherently.

This brings me to the next tools to discuss actually.

- Proof Readers

While I did mention that being a good, successful writer involves being able to type coherently, it's also true that a lot of times we make mistakes. A lot of mistakes! Out of the literal thousands, and thousands of words that exist in just the English language alone, no one person has memorized all of their proper writing, and sometimes to a lot of people there's just little tics and mindsets on how words should be typed out that make sense to us but are generally wrong in how they're really spelled.

This is where the Proof Readers that you have at your disposal really come in handy. In times before computers and electronic typing became a thing, there were actually professional Proofreaders hired by companies whose sole job it was to look at certain manuscripts for any grammatical mistake, spelling mistake, and send it back to the writer to be corrected. While there still are professional proofreaders even now who have that as their sole job and who are good at it, we thankfully have free alternative methods of having our writing proofread via programs that are designed to scan the text that we put in and find spelling mistakes that we've made.

Normally these are included in Text Editing Software, such as the previously two mentioned ones, and they're generally pretty well designed as well as giving you alternative words that you could have possibly intended to write instead. While they won't catch every misspelled word that you make (such as if you write "four" instead of "for") they generally give you a guide that allow you to quickly assess your writing, find your mistakes, and change them till they're correct.

Unlike with the Text Editing Software, there really aren't many different options to discuss as they're pretty much everywhere, widely available, and are often built into your writing programs. However, they often don't assess proper grammar, though, which brings us to the next sort of Proof Reader that you can use.

Grammar Checkers

Proofreaders are good at helping you find mistakes in your spelling. Grammar Checkers are good at finding problems with your grammar and suggesting alternatives to improve them. Often they scan the entire document that you wrote and check for which words are most often used and in what context. If you use a lot of past tense words, the Grammar Checker assumes you're writing in a past tense and will offer alternative ways to write words that aren't in a past tense. Alternatively, if you're writing a subject that's in a first person perspective, Grammar Checkers often check for any possible sentences that are structured in a possible third person perspective and makes suggestions on how to change the sentence to improve it.

Not only that, but they'll often also check manuscripts for improper comma usage, semicolons, and other punctuation marks and suggest alternatives for ending punctuation.

One of the most popular ones that are used widely is a program called "Grammarly" found at the following website:

grammarly.com

The best part of the Grammarly Grammar Checker is that not only is it a standalone program that you can download and use on your desktop like any other sort of text editor program, but it also has extensions and plugins that you can use in your web browser that's used through the Google Chrome and Firefox browser. Used in this way it assesses any sort of writing that you do in any sort of text box that you write in, and shows which corrections should be made, and even offers suggestions.

While this is all well and good and everything for basic writing, it does tend to get in the way of informal writing, which isn't terribly bad. However, one of the problems that Grammarly has is that it doesn't assess the writing itself and tell you which sections are grammatically hard to read, or comprehend, or informs you of too much verb usage and the like.

That's where another application called Hemingway App comes in handy. Found at http://www.hemingwayapp.com/ it's a program that, like Grammarly, can either be downloaded for offline, desktop use or used in the web browser that you find when you load up the website. While Hemingway App is different than Grammarly in that it doesn't assess your manuscript and offer alternative words or corrects your grammar, it does read it and assess it differently.

Essentially what Hemingway App does is it reads your writing and assigns it a readability level, and showcases which sentences are grammatically hard to read, which ones are difficult, which phrases can be simplified, identifies if you're using too many adverbs, and even see's if you're using too much passive voice.

The difference between the two Grammar Checkers though is that Grammarly identifies which sentences are grammatically wrong and offers advice on how to improve while Hemingway App only shows you how hard it is to read. Fundamentally they're completely different and are used in entirely different ways. This helps you by not creating too much overlap.

The best part is, is that they're not the only programs available for use either. There are countless derivatives of these two programs that are in various states of paid, and free. The aforementioned programs are merely just programs that I personally use, so it's up to you, the reader, to research the different programs on your own and even use them to find out which ones work perfectly well for your needs.

But that does bring up an interesting point for another tool that needs to be talked about.

Plagiarism Detection Tools

Plagiarism is a problem, and not in an academic sense. Academically we're told in school that plagiarism is bad because it's essentially stealing someone else's work and passing it off as our own. And when it comes to being a successful writer that still holds true.

There is a massive amount of text out there on the Internet; More than any other medium. Not only is everyone able to be a decent writer with a little bit of practice and knowledge of sentence structures, but with the massive amount of writing that's done on a daily basis it's easy for it to not be seen by more than a dozen people.

And that makes plagiarism one of the easiest things to do. Even if someone's writing isn't seen to a wide audience, theft is theft and doesn't make it right.

Thankfully, there are tools that are designed to combat plagiarism by allowing us to put in any sort of text into the program and checking to see if it was repeated anywhere else on the internet, or even in other written, published works.

Mostly these tools are designed for academic students checking to make sure that their essays and homework is done correctly, and for customers looking to make sure that the book they're reading isn't simply copied from another place, especially if they buy multiple different guides on the same subject. It's also nice to see occasionally as well if anything you've written has been said anywhere else so as to minimize the possibility of theft, accidental or not.

Of course also, keep in mind that this generally doesn't include normal words or phrases that are common in your native languages. Idioms, similes, and common phrases generally aren't considered plagiarized if you include them in your manuscript. And even if you've plagiarized someone's work, it's generally considered acceptable if you quote or otherwise cite your sources.

This brings us to the last tools that you'll possibly be using as well that you can add to your personal writing arsenal.

Word Spinners

Word Spinners are essentially programs that search through your written manuscript and "spin" them. Spinning in this context is defined as changing sentence structure, changing verbs, nouns, and even conjunctions to either synonyms or antonyms. All of this is supposed to generate new and unique content that passes plagiarism detection software.

Keep in mind though that for all the good that Word Spinning software can do, there's also a downside to it that's entirely unethical.

Ethically speaking, it's a nice way to re-write different sentences or paragraphs into completely new and unique ways. Having a problem writing a paragraph and unsure of how to word it? Put it in a word spinner and restructure it a dozen different ways to get an idea of how to re-write. Want to rewrite an earlier blog article and re-use it without simply copy and pasting it? As long as the intellectual property belongs to you, you can easily re-write it how many times you want.

Unethically you can see where this is going. You can take any sort of written topic and "spin it" by rearranging and changing different verbs and nouns to the point that it will easily pass plagiarism detection software, giving the impression that the writing is completely new and original.

The only reason I'm even mentioning that in the first place is that enterprising and lazy writers would end up taking that bit of information and conclude that since it wasn't mentioned, that it must be alright to do just that and pass off another person's writing as yours after you've spun it. That's wrong on several different levels though and is why I'm choosing to include this warning in with this guide.

Stealing is stealing, no matter if you change it around to the point that it's no longer considered plagiarized. There is no ethical reason for theft of another person's words, and any successful writer would not condone those actions, to begin with.

Instead, keep it in mind that Word Spinners are just a nice, easy way to re-write your own written words, and should not be used to steal the words of others.

How does all of this tie in together, though? What's the point of getting all of these different tools that do different things? Mostly it's to help you in the creative process of writing. A lot of times, even as an authority figure on certain subjects, you need to do use research, sources, and stuff to back your claims, and sometimes you also need to use information that you've been given. So the text editing software is good for making sure that you write cleanly consistently, proofreaders are good for making sure that you don't continually make mistakes while writing, since typo's and grammatical mistakes do not look professional, and plagiarism tools are designed to make sure that you're not accidentally copying anyone else (think of them also as a early legal prevention tool as well). Word spinners are also excellent for re-writing your words on the fly if you need to repeat information in another e-book and not sound like you're repeating yourself.

Now the fun part is done. You've gotten your book written, and it's time to actually start formatting it for publication.

CHAPTER 6

FORMATTING YOUR BOOK

So now you've gotten your book entirely written out. You've broken it down into chapters, you've gotten a nice cover image all made up, and you might even have images within the book itself. You've even chosen different fonts and everything and spent more time prettying up the manuscript than you spent writing the thing, to begin with.

What now?

Now you choose which format you wish to publish in. Technically speaking, the KDP format does allow you to upload and publish in a myriad of different formats that include RTF, PDF, TXT, and others, they're not all designed the same and not all of them are all that good for publishing purposes.

So then which format do you go with?

It all depends on what you want out there, and who you want it to be seen by. RTF, TXT. ODT and even DOC formats are nice and simple since they're already based off of the text editing program that you're using. However, the problem that's inherent with them is that they're liable to be quickly copied, pasted, and edited. This isn't a program for some readers, which don't really allow for text modification purposes, and RTF and TXT formats are pretty universal across multiple IOS's (Such as Android or Apple products), but it makes them easier to "steal" and copy and pasted from on computers.

Likewise, some formats such as PDF and HTML don't allow for any of the text to be edited and makes it perfect for distribution.

There is another format though that is unique to the KDP platform called Mobi that allows your manuscript to easily be opened across multiple platforms all at once, so you don't have to worry about installing different programs, or the like. It's actually an interesting format that works well, especially since most people already have the readers installed on their computers, tablets, or reader devices. Plus, it's easy to convert any document to it. in fact, many well off authors who write through the KDP format actually recommend installing in Mobi when using KDP.

How to convert to that format then?

First, download the free programs that are already accessible to you as an author called "KindleGen" and "Kindle Previewer.". These are small programs that are immensely helpful, as KindleGen converts all HTML and other formats into the Mobi format, and Kindle Previewer shows you how you appear on both different versions of kindles, and in different kinds of devices such as smartphones, tablets, and the like. It's an excellent tool that helps you get an idea of what to expect from the perspective of different customers.

That's actually really it, and actually, is one of the most hassle-free aspects of creating your ebook. While there might be some issues that do crop up, such as some formatting options not being compatible with others, or sometimes there being an issue with incompatible fonts and such, it's easy enough fix to modify your manuscript and try again once more.

Now all that's really left is the question of how to publish your eBook. You've got the book written, you've formatted it to mobi (or any other format of your choice), and you've got the KDP account made, and even looked at the Terms of service and options before you. How do you start to publish it?

Chapter 7

Publishing Your Book

Uploading your book and getting it published is actually really simple and hassle free. You'd expect it to be harder to do so, and there to be a review portion where you upload it, and Amazon checks it to see if it's good enough to be published before approving you after a set moderation period, but in all honesty it's only a few button clicks away before you've uploaded it onto their servers, and they enter you into their systems.

First off, once you've started the uploading process you're greeted with various different options to choose from. This is all designed to decide where you want to place your book and have it categorized, since after all if you're writing a book about fishing, you don't want it in the gardening section, and if you're writing a book about gardening you don't want it in video game tips and tricks. Not only that but it also allows potential buyers the chance to find your book browsing through the wide selection that's already there. You're allowed two different categories, which usually have a broad category, with a subcategory beneath it.

From there, you add upwards of up to seven different keywords for your book as well. While it was mentioned before in earlier chapters that 4 is a very good number, to choose from when it comes to choosing keywords, you are allowed up to seven. So if you feel that you need more than four keywords, feel free to put them in now. Although you can change it in the future.

From there, you upload your Cover photo, and then you choose whether or not to have Digital Rights Management Protection. You don't necessarily need this option really since it does impact your potential earnings and everything, but the option is there for you to have and you can choose to turn it on or off in the options if you ever decide to change your mind.

With that said, once you've gone through all the options again and made sure everything was perfectly fitted, you click on the accept button, and it automatically uploads it for you, and within 24 to 48 hours your book will be entered into Amazon's extensive catalog.

Congratulations! If you've done everything so far that this book as recommended up until this point, you've just gone ahead and published your first book. Now, you can sit back, and relax, and wait for the money to come to you, and potential buyers to start purchasing your book.

Of course, you're not completely done just yet. You've actually only just started working in the wonderful world of Kindle Publishing. There's a lot more than meets the eye, and there are extensive background services that need to be done if you really want to start drawing attention to your works.

CHAPTER 8

MARKETING TACTICS FOR INDIE PUBLISHERS

This chapter deals with learning to market yourself. Marketing is something that's vastly important to your success as a writer on the internet. It's not enough that you just produce a little bit of work, build a portfolio, and then expect the customers to come flocking to you. In a perfect world that would happen, where the customers who are looking for you would come and find you, purchase all of your books, and leave positive reviews. Sadly, though, we're not living in a perfect world.

Without marketing yourself prospective customers will have no idea that you even exist, and thus can't find you.

How do you market yourself then?

Luckily with the Internet taking over everyone's lives and becoming the one tool that everyone in all developed nations needs access to, there are a lot of different social media places that you can go to and sign up for that are all free. Everyone in this day and age has a Facebook, a Twitter, a Tumblr, and other artists even have Instagram and other places. That's a large percentage of people when you truly stop to think about it, and you can easily contact them or have a place for them to access and contact you. Naturally, most people won't be looking for a writer for anything, but that doesn't stop businesses, content creators, and even other authors and writers wanting to reach out to connect with Writers for their myriad of different projects.

By having a place and developing an internet presence you essentially put yourself out there to potential customers who will see your work, see what you produce, and potentially want to hire you for their writing needs in the future.

Keep in mind, though, that each different social media website, for the most part, functions completely differently from one another. Let's take a look at some of the more popular places you can go to.

Facebook

Facebook is everywhere. Everyone has a Facebook. My Grandmother has a Facebook and she watches Jeopardy all day and tends to her garden. Even the technologically illiterate have access to a Facebook because it's so easy to use and completely intuitive to your own experiences, and is often a great way to stay in contact with people. As a Writer, this is invaluable for you as you can keep your fans, customers, partners, and potential business up to date on what you're doing that day. You don't have to write about yourself and your daily life, keep in mind, but daily postings on projects, information about pricing, and even samples of personal stuff from time to time will keep you on everyone's minds, and allow you to engage everyone immediately.

Twitter

At 140 characters long, a lot of what could be said with twitter gets a little left out. However what it lacks in length it makes up for in Brevity and is quick to use on smart phone technology. A lot of what it has in common with Facebook is that it's a nice way to keep in contact with customers, fans, and potential business, but the main difference is that it's quick to share information as well. 140 characters go quickly, and when you're keeping people up to date on you and your work you can quickly "tweet" about what you're doing, or thinking, or even share and "retweet" other things that other people have posted.

Tumblr

Tumblr works as a blog and is entirely different than Facebook or Twitter. Instead of using it as a sort of tool to update what you're doing, it's instead more of place to showcase your writing, your more personal thoughts, and to creatively share content with people who follow you. That's not to say it couldn't be used more like a Facebook, or even a Twitter, but it's more designed around writing, disseminating and sharing information, and quickly spreading that throughout a different medium and can be also used by content creators to do the same without having to go to Facebook or the limited numbers of Twitter. Perfect for being used as a backup place to write freely and off the cuff and have people comment, share, and reblog what you've written.

Patreon

Patreon isn't truly a social media platform like the previous three. Instead, what Patreon is a place where content creators, and yes, even writers, can go and update their profiles and keep people up to date with their current projects. In return, people can host you as a "patron" and pledge money to you either on a monthly basis or per a number of projects finished. It's a nice website that's designed more for the creative minded writers out there, and makes for an excellent additional source of income that can easily be shared among all of the fans, and customers that you'll end up having the more you start to become successful. While it's possible to eventually completely become independent and subsist solely on Patreon donations for work, keep in mind that this should not be a plan. As a writer, you'll want to look for several different revenue streams where you're working and not become solely attached to one place.

All in all, though each of the social media websites mentioned is excellent for what they offer, and it's not really a requirement to become involved in all of them. In fact, a lot of successful writers use predominantly only one, with a lot less having two or more websites they post on. Me personally I use really only two: Facebook and Twitter. Facebook because I can post and update and even queue up posts all at once and only attend to it every few days, and twitter because I just write silly little things that come to my mind and people re-tweet or comment on what I had said and I engage an audience in that way.

Try it out, see what every website has to offer you. Some might be perfect for what you need, some perhaps not, and you might even find other social media outlets that cater to your needs as well. Early on, don't be afraid to experiment.

Chapter 9

Scaling And Growing Your Business

By now you should be seeing a steady pace in growth with your eBook business that you've got going on, provided you've at least listened to a lot of the advice that was in this book. You should be getting customers in, purchasing your book, and at least leaving some positive reviews for your products before leaving, and you should also be seeing a steady stream of growing repeat customers who enjoy your books and decide that they want more of what you have to write. As you'll find out, with more success comes (naturally) more income, but there's a large problem with growing a business practically from the ground up. Paradoxically, the more success you earn, the more work you find yourself doing. Unlike a lot of other businesses, when it comes to writing and maintaining a certain level of rate of publishing, you have to remain on the ball and publish at a certain set interval to continue to keep the attention of all your customers. Not only does this give you a larger pool of books to purchase from when new customers find you and like what they see and potentially buy more than a single book, but you're returning customers almost expect you on a schedule to produce something, especially if they feel that whatever you'll write will help.

Not only that, but let's also assume that you've found a perfect system through social media marketing, and connected with your fan base and it's been drawing in a steady stream of attention. Your fans and other customers will continue to expect you to keep developing social media content as well, and update them on upcoming projects that you're working. Plus some websites, such as Patreon, are dependent on you producing content as patrons donate to you in the hopes of either seeing early content or to see you spend more time creating things that they like to see from you.

So it can quickly get out of hand with the amount of work that you're expected to do after you've started seeing success. Your work schedule can go from two to three hours a day to over ten hours easily. How do you cope?

One of the best ways that a lot of experts have found was simply outsourcing your work to freelancers. Hiring out freelancers not only frees your time for other work that needs your immediate attention, but also, allows you produce work at a constant rate or even an increased rate.

Now wait, you might ask. Isn't that technically cheating since you're really only piggybacking off of the writing talent of another person? After all, you've been told plagiarism is bad, and by hiring someone else to produce your written content, design your covers, proofread, or even market, you're essentially plagiarizing their work for your benefit while they don't get anything.

This is only partially true. It's true that if you have someone write something for you and you take it without their permission and sell it, you're guilty of plagiarism, but there's actually laws in place that allow you to do that sort of thing legally.

The thought process of it goes: If you hire someone and outsource your work to them and pay them money not only for their time but the copyright, then you're entitled to that product. In fact, there are contracts that you can write up for any hired freelancer to have them signed that states that any work that they produce belongs to you and becomes your intellectual property once you've exchanged money. This not only protects you and ensures you're getting a product that they can't further profit off of in the future, but also makes sure that they cannot sue you for stealing their property. So it's highly advisable to get a Non-Disclosure Agreement as well as a lawyer for any outsourcing work that you do intend to do.

So then how do you successfully find Freelancers? And if so, how much should you be expected to pay them?

Luckily with the introduction of the Information Age and the Internet becoming a large part of our everyday lives, finding Freelancers is extremely easy. In fact, there are whole communities that have sprung up on the internet devoted to hiring freelancers for a myriad of different things from writing to art, to computer work, to even marketing and finances.

Websites such as Fiverr.com, Freelancer.com, Upwork.com, and a host of others are full of people of varying skill sets that can help you with your writing needs. It's all a matter of signing up, perusing the different profiles of people who want to work, and engaging them in business.

So then what do you pay them?

Often on these Freelance communities, they already have a rate of work displayed, showing what they'll work for, how long they'll work, as well as additional information, including background, revision policies, and possibly even samples of their work. It's all a matter of seeing what your budget is, and finding a writer, or a cover artist who has the skills that match what you're looking for.

Generally though if the website you're looking through doesn't have a charge rate for you to look at? It's generally acceptable to calculate it out to a livable rate. This means factoring in how long it will take them to write what you need, proofreading, editing, and other factors that you either don't want to do or that they'll offer to do. For the most part in the United States, it's considered that $8 per hour of work is, at the least, the minimum that you should hire for. Not only is it dishonest to hire someone at a rate that's not worth the time they put it, but it's also suspicious that someone would choose to work at low rates. More often than not, someone willing to work for far less than they're worth operate a plagiarism scam and is why for every sample you receive you should always double check your sources.

Once you've settled on a price, the parameters of the contract, the due date, and all other necessary options to negotiate, payment is pretty simple after that. If the Freelancer delivers and follows the contract (whether verbal or written), you pay them through the methods that were discussed. It's as simple as that.

Not only will hiring Freelancers help you with your business as you grow, and find you need help in maintaining your business, but you're also helping an industry as well, and by having Freelancers on your payroll that prove to be worthwhile, you'll find that your time is easier managed, and your business will continue to improve, with people around you that you can trust.

Chapter 10

Final Thoughts

All in all, though, what it ultimately comes down to for success is you.

Yes, you.

This guide is perfect for getting you a basic start, though. It's given you at least an outline of things that you need to focus on and work on before you can truly begin and get to work, and it's even given you information about resources and tools at your disposal as well as a wealth of information for different websites outside of the KDP platform. All in all, this guide should just be that for you: A guide, and proof that you can write as a career and find success publishing E-books. After all, you have this book in your hand, and it wasn't written by you. If you paid for it, that should be proof enough, correct?

Still, what this guide cannot do is determine your level of success. That's all dependent on how well you can focus and motivate yourself. Early on you're probably not going to find a lot of success, especially after just starting out. No one comes out of the gates, starting up an account on the KDP platform and publishes 100 books and make $2,000 right off the bat. That sort of level of success takes a lot of time and dedication to cultivate and is earned through sweat, tears, boredom, and striving to be better. Starting out, you're to end up having days where you'll write 10,000 words for an e-book, delete it all, and start over from scratch. You're going to end up with days where you won't see a single purchase, where your impressions will lower; you'll see a 1-star review that critiques your writing, or any number of different things.

Other days you're going to do the same thing, only you find a bit of success. Several people purchasing your books, a few positive reviews, people donating to your patreon, and finding yourself on some sort of list of authors to check out.

Other times, you'll even have enough in your bank account to pay off all your bills, and get a little bit of extra food on the side as well.

If anything can be said, though, keep at it. Learn from your mistakes, focus on your end goal, and continue to keep working. Eventually things will fall into place, and eventually, you'll even find a lot of success by having your books enjoyed outside of a small select group. In fact eventually, you'll probably start to be seen as an authority in the niches you fill, and an authority on writing that all younger writers aspire to me. You might even start seeing yourself expanding from just the Kindle Publishing Platform itself and might even start publishing through normal means.

You just have to stay with it, though, and you have to at all times remain professional, remain humble. Humility is a lifelong lesson, and perseverance is often rewarded.

As we leave this guide, though, I'd like to at least leave you with an inspirational quote that plenty of people draw inspiration from. When you find yourself slacking off when you find yourself making excuses for not working, or when you're not giving it your all, look to this quote and remember that hard times hurt, but inspiration can help lessen that. It's an inspiration that makes you realize that you are the Captain and Commander of your success and that it is all dependent on your drive to succeed.

"If you really want to do something, you'll find a way. If you don't, you'll find an excuse" ~ Jim Rohn

CAN I ASK A FAVOUR?

If you enjoyed this book, found it useful or otherwise then I'd really appreciate it if you would post a short review on Amazon. I do read all the reviews personally so that I can continually write what people are wanting.

If you'd like to leave a review then please head over to the Amazon product page.

Thank you for your support!

BONUS #1

Tips to Starting Your Own Kindle Publishing Business

As a token of my appreciation for purchasing this book, I have decided to add an additional chapter which I think will immensely help you to get started with your own publishing business. As always don't forget to rate and comment and tell me how you liked this book!

TIP 1: PICK YOUR NICHE

When choosing a topic for your book, find a niche that's large enough to generate sufficient sales, while still small enough that you can dominate it. To identify such a niche, generate a list of keywords that best describes your own expertise and then search for books on those topics in the Kindle Store. Stick to UK versions if your book will mainly appeal to natives, otherwise base your analysis on Amazon.com. Start with quite a broad search phrase and narrow it whenever you encounter too many competitors.

For example, you might start by searching for plain "Raspberry Pi" if you're interested in writing about this cheap computing phenomenon.

Sort your results by popularity and then open the top one. When I tried this it was, hardly surprisingly, the official Raspberry Pi User Guide (co-written by Gareth Halfacree of this parish). Its ranking at just over 5,000 suggests sales of at least 15 copies per day at a royalty of £6 per copy, or some £90 per day, £30,000+ per annum from UK sales. Not bad.

Repeat this process by moving down the search list. In this example, the second-most popular title generates around £22 per day and the next few £16, £5 and £2.50 respectively. You'll notice a familiar pattern here, where two-thirds of the revenues go to the most popular title and more than 80% to the top two together. Carry on down some way and you'll very soon be among books that required considerable effort to produce but are selling around one copy a week.

You conclude that there's clearly money to be made from an enthusiastic audience eager to learn, especially considering that you've only looked at UK Kindle sales so far, and many of these titles will be available globally in multiple formats. But you also see plenty of titles in this niche that have failed to make any impact at all.

Tip 2: Publish a Great Book

Having located your market niche, you'll need to produce the goods. Remember to closely base your actual title on the keywords you researched, since this is how your audience will find you on Amazon. This may sound obvious, but if you were to compare the best-selling books in any particular category with those that languish in the virtual equivalent of a box under the bed, you'll notice big differences in quality – the most popular books will be professionally presented, complete and well written.

Having a copy editor run through your book at least once before publishing is an excellent investment, and unless you're a graphic artist you should also hire a cover designer. Many potential readers get no further than the thumbnail, and since the ebook shops don't separate titles into ones published by industry giants and home-produced efforts, your "Guide to Microsoft Office" needs to look the business when viewed alongside similar titles from the big guns.

Fortunately, neither copy-editing nor cover design are particularly expensive: just make sure you pick contractors who are qualified and competent, rather than automatically plumping for the cheapest.
Your book will succeed or fail based on the reviews it receives, so producing a professional package will go a long way to satisfying the fickle ebook audience.

TIP 3: GET THE PRICE RIGHT

Professor Brian Cox discovered just how fickle ebook purchasers can be when he contributed to a book that explains how the universe will end. This was part of a series called "Shorts", and managed to distil a complex subject down into an understandable format for 99p. The problem according to most Amazon reviewers was that he did this in a measly 20 pages. You might think having the end of the universe explained in layman's terms for less than a quid is a bargain, but many Kindle readers disagreed, measuring value based purely on pages per penny.

The rules of print paperback production don't apply to ebooks

This said, the rules of print paperback production don't apply to ebooks, since readers can't judge a Kindle book by its heft in their hand – anything above about 50 pages will usually be considered a reasonable read for a non-fiction book.

When you plan your book, then, consider the right size. I planned to sell my 200-pager for £4.99, but it might have been wiser to split it into four 50-page chunks on different aspects of the topic, then sell each for £1.49. This will work better for some subject matter than others; just remember that the ebook format frees you from any specific page count.

Once your book has been released, experiment with pricing. Mine has dropped from £4.99 at launch to a current price of £1.99. I left it at the high price for a few months, then tested the way changes affect revenue by dropping it to £1.49 over Easter, and finally raised it a little again. Surprisingly, I make much the same money from the book whatever its price, since roughly when I halve the price I double sales. But higher sales bring a better ranking and more reviews, both of which increase credibility and conversion rate, so while the revenue stream may be the same either way, I'd expect sales to last longer at a lower price point.

Tip 4: Multiple media

Writers and publishers have barely started breaking free of the constraints imposed by traditional printing methods, and I expect to see a lot of innovation in connecting together different media over the next few years. Our mythical Raspberry Pi book, for example, might contain links to supporting YouTube tutorials that show how to translate the principles it describes into practice.

For now, one effective way to maximize the return on your writing is to also publish your ebook as a paperback. Print-on-demand services such as Lulu and Amazon's own CreateSpace enable you to offer a paperback version, which can be delivered as quickly as a traditionally published book, since Amazon keeps a small stock. Actually, to Amazon there's no difference between a Lulu-printed book and one from HarperCollins, which regrettably means that it will take the same big chunk of its cover price.

On the other hand, linking your paperback and Kindle book together will drive sales of both, since reviews are amalgamated into a single listing that inevitably makes the ebook look a bargain.

You can also buy copies of your own print book at cost (around £3 each for a 200-page paperback) to sell directly through your own channels, which enables you to keep a much larger slice of the profit. Also consider offering a PDF version of the book direct from your own website, whose cost to you is close to zero.

Tip 5: Find an Audience

It isn't enough to write an excellent book, publish it and hope for the best. If you've done your research and picked a good title, some readers searching on Amazon will certainly find you, but you need to supplement them with direct traffic from other sources if you're to make the most of your hard work. One approach is to sell your book directly as I just mentioned: if you have an established website with an appropriate audience, consider both selling the printed version and including links to the Kindle version.

You can also tap an existing community for valuable marketing information. I asked the customers of my retail craft business what they wanted covered in my book and was surprised by their replies: my book was all the better for their direct input. I promised a free copy of the ebook to all who contributed, then emailed to ask for their reviews once they'd read it. Frankly I was disappointed by that response, as the 100 contributors wrote only a couple of reviews between them. For my next book I'll be looking at strategies for getting more reviews that are available on publication day, since these strongly influence sales.

Google+ recently introduced "Communities", a feature that allows like-minded people to discuss related topics in a far more sophisticated manner than Facebook's Pages or Groups. If you were writing a book about, say, Raspberry Pi, there are several communities devoted to that device you can join – contribute to them and you earn the right to gently promote your book from time to time.

My experience was that income from KDP Select lending outstripped combined revenues from the Apple, Barnes & Noble and Kobo stores

Communities are also a great place to learn more about your subject – including self-publishing itself (check out the APE:

Authors, Publishers, Entrepreneurs) – particularly in fast-moving fields. I think Communities may prove to be the killer feature of Google+, with much of the social network's interaction taking place in these super-forums. I'll also be more actively building an email list for my next book – which, after all, is what I'd do for any other product or business.

TIP 6: STICK TO ONE PLATFORM

This one's simple: don't bother with any other ebook platform until you've nailed Kindle Direct Publishing (KDP). Even then, think carefully about whether your time will be well spent – I've described previously the tortuous hoops I was put through to get my title published on Apple's iBookstore, Barnes & Noble's Nook and the Kobo store. That was an utter waste of time I could otherwise have spent either promoting sales on KDP or writing another book.

Perhaps I shouldn't have been so surprised since – in the case of Apple's devices – readers have the option to use the Kindle app rather than iBooks. The market for Nook and Kobo books seems tiny compared with that for Kindle, and I'd only bother if you've exhausted all avenues to increase sales on Amazon's platform.

Sticking exclusively to KDP qualifies your title for the KDP Select program, which enables you to offer your book free for a specified number of days in order to drum up interest and generate reviews. Perhaps more significantly still, it means your ebook can be borrowed by Kindle-owning members of Amazon's Prime program. You'll be paid each time someone borrows your book, and while the amount isn't huge (around £1 per loan), my experience was that income from KDP Select lending outstripped combined revenues from the Apple, Barnes & Noble and Kobo stores.

Tip 7: One Niche, Multiple Titles

I haven't tested this tip yet, but I've come across it many times during my research. It makes sense that if a reader likes your book they may well enjoy other books by you – but only so long as they cover a similar topic. This works with fiction too: I'd buy anything by Terry Pratchett within the genre for which he's famous, but if he published a book of romantic fiction I'd be off like a shot.

If your interests are too wide to accommodate within one genre, then take another tip from fiction and consider using a pen name for your other titles. However, from a business point of view, you ought to stick to a single niche, allowing you to offer book bundles, and even give away the first title in a series to drive sales of the rest. You can also cross-promote books, and the more titles you have, the more effective this will be.

Using these tips, I've made more money (both in revenue and profit) from one book over three months than from my entire stable of mobile apps in a year, and with far less time invested. Not surprisingly, then, I'll be experimenting further with self-publishing for profit over the coming year, and will keep you up to date.

Bonus #2

How To Market Your Kindle Ebooks

The elementary principles of marketing and promotion are pretty much identical for an e-book as for a tangible book. When marketing e-books, it's ideal to do it online. There are quite a few nice strategies to assist you in this extremely important process.

Pricing makes a huge difference. Having a general understanding of what is actually selling in the market helps to make sure you're reasonably within the competitive range.

Here are the average prices of various kinds of works on Amazon:

- The average price of a hardcover book on Amazon is about $9.99
- Books that are on the market as trade soft covers often are priced from $5.99 to $7.99 as the Kindle editions
- Big market paperbacks generally cost around $2.99-$4.99
- Monthly subscriptions to magazines and newspapers are within the range of $9.99$14.99
- One magazine issue is within the $1.49-$2.99 range
- Some big name magazines are about ½ price of offline subscriptions
- Blog monthly subscriptions are about $0.99 with a typically free 14-day trial

- Articles that are by themselves and other short form works are $0.99-$2.99

How to Choose a Price

Theoretically, the lower the price on a book, the higher the conversion rate should be. Similar to selling products on websites, people have to know that your site exists as the first step; you can have the most sophisticated, creative, and high quality site out there, but if people have no idea it exists, what good is it? This concept works identically with e-books.

Here are some pricing tips for works you're selling:

- For diminutive length stories or works or articles, price it from $0.99 to $2.99
- For books, start low and change as needed
- It is highly suggested to not charge more than $9.99 for a usual novel-length book
- Softcover books should run from $2.99-$7.99
- Books only available in digital form should be priced with good judgment
- Depending on the niche your book is in, it may get by with being more expensive than the standard price; usually, these kinds of books deal with something very scientific, are saturated with a lot of graphics, or may be justified if you have to reimburse people who helped with the work.

Amazon Sales Rank

Amazon shows how great a work is performing via the sales ranking system. It's modified by the hour and is computed based on current and past sales information. In order to thin down a product's sales results, items are graded by how great they are performing in their solo niches with category sales ranks.

Standard sales rank is different because it displays how great a product is selling as a big picture. Only writers publishing via the KDP can see their sales reports in their own accounts.

How Sales Rank Works

The more people purchase your product in the Kindle store, the higher chances your work will become very recognizable in your niche. The more sales you make, the more exposure your work will get. It will be difficult to make it to the top ten, but even if you make it to the top 100 or even 500, your exposure and sales will enhance tremendously.

Customer reviews hold a high significance on book sales; poor reviews usually decrease book sales and positive reviews are the prerequisite to people telling their friends, family, and acquaintances about how great your work was, meaning a lot more sales!

Transitioning into paper books

If it happens that you decide to release a title solely for the Kindle but later put forward a Print on Demand edition of that book, the sale information and review assessments for the e-book edition diffuse into the print version that is sold in the standard Amazon book store section of the site.

To ensure the formatting of your book is pleasant in the Print on Demand version, check out CreateSpace; to find it online, just put in "createspace" in the Amazon search bar to pull it up. **CreateSpace** is a supplementary company to Amazon. When you see the page, it'll allow you to register and submit works for no charge.

When you make a Print on Demand title, CreateSpace gives a free ISBN if you don't have it at the time of registering. After you acquire this number, you may use it for your current Kindle title so that the two will be connected together on Amazon.

Promotions

There are a multitude of methods to promote your eBook. Here are some strategies to use in introducing your new work:

- It is ideal, since you're a new author and have to prove yourself to your audiences, to start with a cheap introductory price like $0.99. After your book picks up the pace in sales and become trendier, you can increase the price slowly as time goes on.
- If you have a long length book, it is worth a shot to put up a small excerpt of it as being available for sale as a teaser that will persuade readers to purchase the book in its whole form. If you have a non-fiction book, you can pull out a small section of content that is very helpful, abstract, and/or not well known.

If you wrote a fiction book or other fiction based work, take an excerpt from a very exciting part of the book where it's from an escalated action point or some other highlight. The bottom line is that whatever people read in the excerpts showcased, should really incite a strong desire to read the rest of it. Excerpts run from $0.99-$2.49 and are about the length of an article from 1-5 pages.

Serializing Your Work

If you have a work (non-fiction or fiction) that is very lengthy, it's a good idea to chop it up into sections and sell them apart from each other. As a guideline, think of novelettes from about 7,000-18,000 words; novellas from around 18,000-40,000 words; books/novels as 40,000+ words.

The most important point to remember is that in your series, every chapter should be able to stand on its own "two legs," meaning that the end of the chapter should leave a cliffhanger where it begs the reader to want to read the next chapter. The Charles Dickens' books are an example of successful serialized series.

It's up to you if you prefer to finish the work completely and then start serializing it, or if you prefer to write it as you progress. After your e-book is serialized from beginning to end, you may publish it as one volume. Taking the approach of serializing can be beneficial for the promotion of your work because it can build up curiosity and eagerness while creating a flame around the series.

All of these traits can assist in wheeling in new readers. If your work qualifies as bringing in the heat to readers, it might be able to mainly rely on people telling others about it and social marketing advertisement.

Press Release

Putting out a press release may be worth a shot to include in your marketing portfolio; it could help market your e-book mainly if you're a resident in a small to medium sized city. This may help because you would be a local resident publishing a book, which may be considered exciting and attention-grabbing.

Your home-based radio stations, newspapers, and television channels might become interested in an article or interview; this exposure would be just what you need to market your book in your town. Be very methodical in choosing the newspapers or television stations you'll target by doing research on them to see if what you will offer will have a higher chance of creating interest to that station.

For example, if you are writing a book about how weather affects people's moods and health, choosing weather stations to target would be a logical decision. Don't just pick and submit to many stations without doing your homework. It is a good idea to write a cover letter to a specific person with a press release or phone call.

How to Social Network Offline

To network efficiently means to keep an eye and ear open to latest opportunities. Try your best to make the most of what opportunity comes your way, meaning how you can advertise your work in your community and in other avenues.

It is helpful to start by looking at the topic your work is about to choose where it could fit, i.e. If your work is regarding the history of reptiles, you could see if there are any zoos, aquariums, and museums in your area to tell your book about. There could also be an animal appreciation group that might be interested in promoting your e-book.

If you're a newcomer to the sport of publishing, you might want to read industry works similar to your genre, i.e. if your niche is in healthy food, check out reading magazines such as Cooking Light and other related publications so you can be familiar with similar groupings and organizations.

You could take an extract from your work and send an article to them as well. If your article is approved and published, you can request the editor to put a note that the article is selected from your Kindle book, and tag on the title and a url to the work. Be open minded with trying various ideas and always be on the lookout for promoting opportunities.

Relatives and Friends

It can't be stressed enough how important it is to let as many people know about your book via word of mouth. You just never know how its influence can affect your work immensely. Let your family and friends know all about it via a well written email! They have contacts that they can send the email to and a snowball effect can happen.

Business Contacts and Professional Groups

It's a good idea to converse with your professional associates and co-workers when it's fitting to do so; a great idea is to throw a festival to rejoice in the introduction of your Kindle work. Invite workers to the party who have a matching interest to your work's topic. Think about visiting conferences with your work's industry alliances.

Take a couple of tangible copies of your book or a paper ad for your Kindle version to give out to people. Keep in mind that you should be very cautious about how you approach this kind of advertising while conversing with people. You should NOT be very pushy and force your work on anyone; it's considered unprofessional and this act could backfire and give you a horrible reputation—think of it like a website being designated as spam.

The key is to time when and how to act, i.e. if you trade contact information with an editor or publisher, be sure to contact them again in a suitable amount of time and write a sophisticated kind of letter that reminds them of your meeting so you can make sure they remember the correct person. Visit a few conferences if possible. Be vigilant in your networking and learning more data.

You may also get more involved by volunteering in some conferences; you can assist in planning one or put on your creative thinking caps and participate in some other form for a professional society. By doing this, you will get "brownie points" and not be ignored for your efforts, thus helping your reputation.

If you're timid, you are going to have to realize that you have to put yourself out there. Think of it like acting. Practice acting to help ease into the process. It may help you out first to start assisting with things that need it at first to ease yourself into it. Speak to people and trade business cards when the chance happens.

Professional Image

Two groups that are great for published writers to join because they supply a multitude of professional related assets are PEN and The Author Guild. The Author's Guild supports different and important issues for published authors like law-based services, rights' protection, and just reimbursement.

A part of this membership's obligation is that book authors must have a work from an American publisher that is reputable and who obtains a percentage of the work's sales with a large advance in which the writer is the copyright owner.

Unfortunately, if you only have a work on the Kindle, you don't qualify; however, if you signed a royalty contract on your Kindle work with a reputable American publisher that has offered a major advance, then you would meet the criteria. Bear in mind that this type of situation happening is very improbable. Other types of writers that may qualify are contributors, translators, coauthors, ghostwriters, and freelance writers.

PEN promotes open expression as its main foundation. According to its website, its members have published at least two books of "literary character or one book of exceptional distinction."

Here are some websites to some qualified societies that will help guide you:

- The Creative Penn: www.thecreativepenn.com
- John August Screenwriting Tips: http://johnaugust.com
- The Reading Edge Podcast: http://thereadingedge.com
- TeleRead: www.teleread.org ☐ PEN: www.pen.org
- The Authors Guild: www.authorsguild.org
- The Graphic Artists Guild: www.graphicartistsguild.org
- Publetariat: People Who Publish: www.publetariat.com

Blog Marketing

Remember that just having a mind blowing novel on Kindle does not mean you'll automatically be triumphant and become rich. After your publisher has verified your account and it's ready to go, then you'll have the ability to blog right from Author Central for free by checking out the Blog tab. You can blog using two different methods; one method is to go to the "Add an RSS feed" tab and put in the feed address, NOT the blog's address.

Or, you can click the Create a new post address and put in a fresh post straight to Amazon via the box that generates. To make an RSS feed using Blogger, visit your blog to sign in and click Customize at the top. Check that the "Layout" tab is chosen and go to the link "Add a Gadget." Next, include the "subscription links" tool to your blog.

Then, perform all the actions the directions state for initiating this process, which are easy as pie. This is the way to get a RSS subscription capacity included in your blog. To locate your RSS feed address, check out the blog subscription url, which is on your blog's home page.

Click on the url and find "posts;" then, choose how you want your feed to look in its layout from the options given. The next page will showcase your feed address in a url. Copy and paste this url in the proper box at Author Central to begin extracting your blog feeds into your Author Central account. There will be a note giving caution that it may take up to 24 hours for brand new posts to appear on your author page.

Videos

Amazon has a very cool feature that lets authors upload videos. Go to the "videos" tab to upload your work. The following formats are what is accepted to upload videos in: .wmv, .flv, .mpg, .mov, and .avi. A huge advantage to putting up a video on your author page would be for credibility and helping to subtly market your book, i.e. if you performed speaking expeditions, these will look great for your profile.

Another option would be to upload a video of yourself talking about your work without giving away too much to ruin it, the reasons for writing your work, and other things about your work that will incite excitement and suspense. There is something about seeing someone express their passion in "person" vs. on paper alone that allows the reader to absorb it as well.

Amazon permits files that are at the biggest 500 MB. You should go to the "content guidelines" url to check that your video meets the content qualifications. Making a video is not as complicated as it may sound because most new computers come with a built-in camera. Videorecording functions differ depending on the computer.

You can start by doing a search on your computer using the keywords "video" or "camera." If you don't have a camera built into your computer, then you can buy a latest webcam for as low as $8 from www.buy.com. You can also check out www.amazon.com to see if it has cheap webcams.

Cameras are diverse, so you should invest some time in reading the directions to learn how to set it up and record appropriately. Trust me; this'll save you a lot of heartache down the road if you just learn how to do it the right way from the start.

Take heed to the kinds of content Amazon does not allow to be posted:

- Obscene content or things that are offensive like nasty language or depicting other people in a bad way
- Promotions or advertisements
- Stuff that isn't yours to use
- Personal data like phone numbers, mailing addresses, and website urls
- Data on buying and shipping stuff, costs, and other things related

- Commentary to information that is accessible on your author page and within book reviews
- Promotions for good reviews and votes
- Plot spoilers (why would you want to do that anyway?!)

Happenings

After your account is ready to go, you'll be able to put facts regarding your speaking events, speeches, book tours, when you'll be in bookstores, and other happenings under the "events" tab. Amazon is a joint venture partner with a company called book tour: www.booktour.com They follow author occurrences, so all new events you put in your author central page will be distributed with Book Tour; book tour also gives your info to other sites/resources to give you further exposure.

To submit a new happening, go to the "create new event" section and input your description of the event, the location, the name of the work the event is correlated with, and the date and the time it'll begin. Make sure to be very specific and use loads of details as you can in the description section.

Definitely state if you'll be giving a speech on your book or similar topics because this will give you a wonderful chance to squeeze in advertising copy; the key is for it to be pertinent to the book and event bordering it. What you put in the description section needs to seduce readers into attending your event; events are a fabulous way to get exposure and demonstrate that you're involving yourself as a professional in the marketing of your work.

More on Blogs

Creating a name for yourself on the Internet is of vital importance. Amazon has a blog option as mentioned earlier, but it's relatively limited to the amount of exposure you can acquire than if you have a standard blog with one of the biggest free blog services on the net---WordPress and Blogger.

You can check these out by visiting:

http://wordpress.com

Or www.blogger.com

There is a big caveat to using a blog. You need to be honest with yourself and ask if you would want to keep posting to your blog at least once a week. A blog's main purpose is to give consistent updates and if you're not going to do that, there is no point in setting one up. It's simple to run a blog, so that's a good thing.

Here's an example of a fantastic blog by the author Anne Mini below. Read her biographic information as well to get an idea how some of these concepts stated in this book tie together. www.annemini.com. This blog contains an immense amount of helpful information that Anne wrote about grammar guidelines, manuscript layout help, and tons of other things dealing with editing, writing, and the ever evolving realm of publishing.

Your blog does not need to just focus only on your work; you can write about your experiences with your path to publishing for the Kindle, problems you may have ran into (more than likely, others can relate), overall experiences with e-publishing, marketing your work, and other various experiences with agents, editors, or publishers.

Other ideas for topics include writing about your specialize subject of comfort and a multitude of other experiences you have on a professional level of writing. Doing this will help you form a professional profile and reputation that will only enhance your future sales.

Website

Before thinking about investing funds into magazine advertisement, you should first invest money and time into a website instead. It's important to have one because so much information about yourself, works, etc can be put on there. It's ideal to have your website and blog all on one site, within the same domain name.

It is basically like your public identity as an author and a place that readers can easily check out for sources to things linked to your professional profile and work; it also helps that if someone wants to reach you that your contact info is on your site. You never want people to work too hard to be able to find you online because chances are that they will just give up and forget about it. Make it as easy as possible for people to find you online.

For some tips on what to put on your site, it helps to look at how others did it first to get an intuitive idea. It will be easiest just to hire a freelancer or friend to build one for you too on www.elance.com Here are some useful links that can help give you a lot of ideas.

www.kevinprufer.com/index.html

www.mdbell.com

www.stephenking.com

www.how-to-build-websites.com/lessonOne.php

Suggested Information to Include on your website

- Cover graphics
- ISBN
- Summary of work
- Publication date
- Target readership
- Teaser excerpt from the first chapter
- Info about how and where to purchase your book (Make sure this is clear and easy to follow)
- Commentary of your works
- Summaries of each work you've published

- Promotional excerpts by other people in the business
- Don't interweave information; this means to separate your author biographic data from your personal or other non-author career data. The exception is if your job relates to being an author, i.e. if you're a librarian.
- Put in future dates and a chart of previous events like lecture or book tours (that you've attended or are scheduled to attend) that occurred.

As a final reminder, it's very important to keep the material on your site fresh and update at least once a week. If you find yourself in a position to not have anything to think of writing, post news and events in the business from around the internet, or your feedback to a work you've read lately. Just be in the habit (which will put your readers in the habit of checking out your site) of doing this and it'll be easy to continue after a while.

Aside from keeping readers keeping up with what you're doing, it's vital to having a lot of content on your site because this will increase the number of other sites that will link to your site; this linking is very helpful in helping to rank your site in the search engines. Making a positive impression with Google can never hurt, since it's the biggest search engine at the moment.

Now, you have a great starting point to begin your quest to becoming an accomplished author on Kindle. There are many resources available to help. Go for it!

About The Author

Craig is a writer, author, entrepreneur, life coach, personal trainer, speaker and an avid traveler.

Craig has been making money online since 2013 and decided to hop on to Kindle and share with the world his wealth of knowledge. Craig loves the luxury of being able to travel and yet make money doing so.

He always tells his clients, you don't need to think of travelling as an expense but rather as an investment.

Some of his hobbies include:

- Meditation, Mindfulness and The Meaning of Life
- Running, Biking, Swimming, Rock Climbing
- Helping Individuals Reach Their Full Potential
- Spending Time With His Family
- Playing Competitive Basketball
- Writing, Traveling, Blogging

www.ingramcontent.com/pod-product-compliance
Lightning Source LLC
Chambersburg PA
CBHW060415190526
45169CB00002B/903